50 Quick and Brilliant
Teaching Ideas

By Mike Gershon

About the Author

Mike Gershon is a teacher, trainer and writer. He is the author of twenty books on teaching, learning and education, including a number of bestsellers, as well as the co-author of one other. Mike's online resources have been viewed and downloaded more than 2.5 million times by teachers in over 180 countries and territories. He is a regular contributor to the Times Educational Supplement and has created a series of electronic CPD guides for TES PRO. Find out more, get in touch and download free resources at www.mikegershon.com

Training and Consultancy

Mike is an expert trainer whose sessions have received acclaim from teachers across England. Recent bookings include:

- *Improving Literacy Levels in Every Classroom*, St Leonard's Academy, Sussex

- *Growth Mindsets, Effective Marking and Feedback* Ash Manor School, Aldershot

- *Effective Differentiation,* Tri-Borough Alternative Provision (TBAP), London

Mike also works as a consultant, advising on teaching and learning and creating bespoke materials for schools. Recent work includes:

- *Developing and Facilitating Independent Learning,* Chipping Norton School, Oxfordshire

- *Differentiation In-Service Training,* Charles Darwin School, Kent

If you would like speak to Mike about the services he can offer your school, please get in touch by email: mike@mikegershon.com

Other Works from the Same Authors

Available to buy now on Amazon:

How to use Differentiation in the Classroom: The Complete Guide

How to use Assessment for Learning in the Classroom: The Complete Guide

How to use Questioning in the Classroom: The Complete Guide

How to use Discussion in the Classroom: The Complete Guide

How to Teach EAL Students in the Classroom: The Complete Guide

More Secondary Starters and Plenaries

Secondary Starters and Plenaries: History

Teach Now! History: Becoming a Great History Teacher

The Growth Mindset Pocketbook (with Professor Barry Hymer)

How to be Outstanding in the Classroom

Also available to buy now on Amazon, the entire 'Quick 50' Series:

50 Quick and Brilliant Teaching Ideas

50 Quick and Brilliant Teaching Techniques

50 Quick and Easy Lesson Activities

50 Quick Ways to Help Your Students Secure A and B Grades at GCSE

50 Quick Ways to Help Your Students Think, Learn, and Use Their Brains Brilliantly

50 Quick Ways to Motivate and Engage Your Students

50 Quick Ways to Outstanding Teaching

50 Quick Ways to Perfect Behaviour Management

50 Quick and Brilliant Teaching Games

50 Quick and Easy Ways to Outstanding Group Work

50 Quick and Easy Ways to Prepare for Ofsted

50 Quick and Easy Ways Leaders can Prepare for Ofsted

About the Series

The 'Quick 50' series was born out of a desire to provide teachers with practical, tried and tested ideas, activities, strategies and techniques which would help them to teach brilliant lessons, raise achievement and engage and inspire their students.

Every title in the series distils great teaching wisdom into fifty bite-sized chunks. These are easy to digest and easy to apply – perfect for the busy teacher who wants to develop their practice and support their students.

Acknowledgements

As ever I must thank all the fantastic colleagues and students I have worked with over the years, first while training at the Institute of Education, Central Foundation Girls' School and Nower Hill High School and subsequently while working at Pimlico Academy and King Edward VI School in Bury St Edmunds.

Thanks also to Alison and Andrew Metcalfe for a great place to write and finally to Gordon at KallKwik for help with the covers.

Table of Contents

Try a Dance Routine

Washing Line

Wheel of Fortune

Lesson Menu

Swap Classes

Make a Mark

Question Delivery

Say it Together

Jam and Marmalade

Beginning. Middle. End.

Beat the Teacher

Secret Mission

Begin with a Story

Choose Someone to Answer

Bounce

Lego

Plenary Dice

Make Your Own AFL Box

Classtools.net

Sponge Ball

Dingbats

Find the Mistakes

Film Yourself Introducing an Activity

Introduction

Welcome to '50 Quick and Brilliant Teaching Ideas.'

This book is all about providing you with fantastic practical ideas you can use to enhance your teaching. Every entry is different but every single one can be a brilliant addition to your existing toolkit of strategies, activities and techniques.

The emphasis throughout is on creativity. Not only will these ideas bring innovation to your lessons, but in many cases they'll help your pupils to think more creatively as well.

Each of the ideas can be applied across the curriculum and used with different age groups.

And don't forget that all of the ideas can be adapted, changed and developed to suit your teaching style and the needs of your students.

I hope you enjoy the book and find the ideas great additions to your practice. From one teacher to another, read on and be inspired!

Lesson Plan Flow-Chart

01 Sometimes lesson planning can feel like a drag. So much to do and so many ideas buzzing around your head. Or maybe the ideas have all buzzed off because it's been a long day and you're staring at a blank computer screen.

You can make lesson planning easier by drawing out a flow-chart and then filling it in, bit-by-bit, either with the activities or the content you want to put into the lesson. This way, you break up the task, give yourself a sense of how the lesson will move from one thing to another, and make life that little bit easier.

You can get a free flow-chart template here:

http://www.docstoc.com/docs/35019301/Flow-Chart-Model

Say, Do, Think, Write, Reflect

02 Just what are those students going to do in our lessons? There are so many possibilities it can be overwhelming. We could have them recreating the sacking of Rome or performing a Shakespearean monologue. Anything is possible.

But sometimes we just want an effective approach which can make our planning simpler.

So why not try this? Ask yourself what you want students to say, do, think, write and reflect on during your lesson. You might even plan it in that order – discussion first, then activities combined with thinking, followed by writing and all topped off by reflection. Try it out; see if it makes your planning simpler and easier.

Striking Images

03 Today, with the internet at our fingertips, it's easy to get hold of brilliant images which can spark off student thinking. You can use them at the start of lessons, as mid-lesson surprises or even put them on hand-outs. Here are five sites I've found to be great for getting hold of striking images:

- http://www.theguardian.com/world/series/eyewitness
- http://photography.nationalgeographic.co.uk/photography/
- http://www.gettyimages.co.uk/
- http://pictures.reuters.com/
- http://www.loc.gov/pictures/

Ask an Amazing Question

04 Go on, you know you want to. Amazing questions are like Chemistry lessons – they usually get a reaction (groan).

Firing off an amazing question can bring a lesson to life. It can help students to think about things in a completely different light. Or it can totally alter the course of the learning.

Start a Word document and save all the amazing questions you think of there. Have it ready to hand so you can use it when you want. And why not share it with your colleagues – they'll have their own amazing questions you can add to your list as well.

Bring in a Mystery Object

05 A lesson is going to be memorable if it starts off with a mystery object. I can still remember being at primary school and the teacher bringing in items from the Second World War. And that was quite a few years ago now (please don't ask how many).

All subjects have ample opportunities for relevant mystery objects. Have a look through your upcoming lessons and see when and where you might be able to throw something in. Your students will remember it for a long time to come.

Teach from the Back

06 Every day we stand at the front of the class. Every day our students sit there and look up at us. Even if we are doing really active, independent lessons, we still have a few minutes where we stand at the front and give instructions.

Mix things up by teaching from the back. Stretch those legs of yours and take a meander through the classroom. Hit the far side of the room and start things off from there. You'll get a new perspective and so will your students (especially any who are trying to hide out on the back row).

No Chairs and Tables

07 This one really depends on who you are. I mean, if you're teaching PE or Drama then you'll be pretty used to not having any chairs or tables.

If you're doing another subject though, think of the possibilities...

The Geography room becomes a walking tour of New York City; the History classroom transforms into the battlefields of Agincourt; or maybe you just create a really nice space in which pupils can work actively and in groups.

Oh, and one other thing. Some students can't stand working at desks but know they have to get on with it. So taking the chairs and tables away will motivate them and get them on side.

Line Them Up

08 In many lessons we come across things which we could place on a continuum or on a line. For example: a list of dates, parts of a process or events in a play.

You can get your students thinking actively, talking about the content and highly engaged by handing out a set of sheets containing the different dates, parts of the process, events or whatever else, and then asking them to arrange themselves in a line, with each pupil holding a different sheet.

A little bit of chaos might ensue (especially at first) but the end result should make it all worthwhile.

Pack Your Lunchbox

09 When I was at school I used to love opening up my lunchbox to see what I had to eat that day. As I grew a bit older I started making my own lunchbox, putting in all my favourite things. This made lunchtimes even better.

Present your students with a range of tasks connected to the lesson topic and ask them to pack their lunchboxes. Divide the tasks into 'sandwiches,' 'fruit,' 'drinks' and 'snacks.' Explain that pupils must choose one from each, but which they choose is up to them.

Students can then work through the tasks individually or they can team up with others who have made the same choices.

Spot the Lie!

10 This is a really neat activity you can use at any time but which I have found to be best suited to the beginning or the end of lessons. It was first shown to me by José, a former colleague who taught Spanish and it works as follows:

Present your class with six statements connected to the topic you have been studying. Four of these should be true and two should be false. It is up to students to work out which are which and to explain why.

You can vary the level of difficulty by making the lies harder or easier to spot – it just depends how much you want to challenge your pupils.

Choose Something to Mark For

11 All this talk of being in the classroom and we haven't yet mentioned what we need to do afterwards. No, I don't mean go to the staffroom for a cup of tea and a biscuit. I'm talking about marking.

Sometimes marking can lose a bit of its effectiveness. We find ourselves leafing through books, making sure everything is up-to-date and as we expect.

Instead of this, you could try choosing something specific to mark for and then concentrating on this in every book you look at. You might mark for use of keywords, for example, or accuracy of answers.

Whatever you choose, it will help to focus your marking, making it more effective as a result.

Make an Electronic Markbook

12 And while we're at it on marking, let me extol the virtues of electronic markbooks. These are really easy to make. Simply open up an Excel spreadsheet, insert the names of your students and away you go.

The big advantage is that you can use the data simply and easily whenever you're working on a computer – for example by copying and pasting into emails or reports.

In addition, and if you know about these things, you can create graphs and tables which visualise the data you have on your classes. If you are uncertain about how to do this, ask a colleague from the IT department in your school to show you how.

Questions in the Corridors

13 Does learning start and stop at the door of your classroom? Maybe. Does it have to? Maybe not.

A killer question in the corridor can get students talking and thinking all the way to their next lesson, or even right through break time.

You can ask questions while stood at your door in between lessons; while walking the corridors at break; or even before school starts when students are milling about. Just make sure the questions are big, open-ended and exciting – exactly what we want to get those cogs whirring.

Art on the Walls

14 Mix your wall displays up so that student work sits side-by-side with work created by the greatest artists in history. This will send really powerful messages to your pupils, telling them that such high culture is accessible and available to them, and that they can aspire to create work which is similarly at the very limits of what they can do.

You can buy prints from most art galleries (or do it more cheaply by getting a calendar and cutting out the different images).

Alternatively, you can find images of many great artworks online. Simply print these off, laminate them and then stick them on your walls.

Scattegories

15 This is originally a board game from Hasbro. It works as follows when adapted for the classroom:

The teacher chooses six categories and writes these on the board. The categories could all be connected to the topic of study or you could have a mixture (say four connected to the topic and two fun ones).

Students get into teams of three or four. The teacher chooses a letter and calls this out. Now the race is on! Who can be the first team to get a word or phrase for each category which begins with that letter? When a team thinks they have finished, they call out and have their answers checked.

Repeat as many times as you like with different letters.

Target Trackers

16 We all know that giving good, achievable targets which are clear and well-explained is one of the best ways to help students make great progress.

Sometimes though, we can lose track of these targets. So too can our pupils.

An easy way to avoid this happening is to create a sheet on which students can track their targets. Simply create a table with space to write in targets and ask pupils to stick this in the front of their books.

Now, every time students receive a new target they have a place to write it – and they can go back and check how they are getting on any time they like.

Reflective Paragraphs

17 Getting students to think about thinking is no easy task. If we can manage it though, research suggests it will bring significant benefits.

Reflective paragraphs are one way to do it.

Ask pupils to write a paragraph reflecting on their learning, on the thinking they have done, or on whether or not they have met their targets (and why). You might like to follow this up by having students discuss in pairs what they have written.

A really nice technique involves asking pupils to write their target at the start of a piece of work, to try to put it into practice during the work, and then to write a reflective paragraph at the end.

Learning Diaries

18 This is a different way in which to help students reflect on and keep track of their learning.

Create a diary which pupils can use to write reflectively about their learning and thinking. They could do this every lesson, every few lessons or even just a couple of times a term.

You can make a learning diary by creating the pages on Word or PowerPoint, printing them out and then photocopying them into a booklet. Alternatively, you can ask students to write their diary entries in the back of their exercise books.

Radar Charts

19 Radar charts are those charts which look a bit like a cross between a spider's web and a blob of paint. Take a look at some by searching 'radar chart' on Google Image Search.

You can create radar charts for your students to fill in, helping them to reflect on their learning and progress.

Your chart might have categories connected to what you have been studying, to specific skills, or to habits which are the keys to success.

Pupils can fill one in, stick it in their books and then come back to it at a later date to see how far they have progressed.

SMART Targets

20 I know all your targets are smart. This is because you are smart. And you would only set smart targets; no silly targets coming from you!

SMART targets are slightly different. SMART stands for:

- Specific
- Measurable
- Attainable
- Relevant
- Time-Bound

Setting targets with these five key factors in mind helps to ensure you maximise the effectiveness of your targets. You can even teach the method to your pupils so that they can set SMART targets for themselves.

Try a Dance Routine

21 And so we move from the prosaic to the…pretty random!

But why not?

What are dance routines all about?

Fun; co-ordination; effort; learning from mistakes; concentration; working as part of a group; discipline.

If you have a long lesson, take five minutes out in the middle to try a dance routine with your students. They will be energised, surprised, excited and engaged. And they will definitely remember the lesson – along with the learning that went with it.

Washing Line

22 Take a piece of string or rope and tie it across your classroom so that it stretches from one side to the other. Make sure this substitute washing line is hanging from the ceiling and sufficiently high so that it does not distract of impede students.

You now have a great tool to support learning. Things you can attach to the washing line include:

- Questions
- Pupils' Work
- Parts of a process or event
- Pictures
- Keywords

These can be referred to and used during the course of the lesson – either by yourself or by your students.

Wheel of Fortune

23 It seems quite some time since the heyday of the television quiz show 'Wheel of Fortune.' Do not fear, Fortune fans, because the memory of that great game show lives on in this teaching idea.

Make your own wheel of fortune by attaching a circular piece of cardboard to a piece of wood. Write the names of your students on the wheel or write on a range of categories about which you could ask questions.

During lessons, spin the wheel so as to select pupils at random to answer your questions or so as to select random categories about which to ask questions (remember to stick an arrow on the piece of wood – this then indicates the student or category which has been chosen).

Lesson Menu

24 Being presented with a menu is a pleasant experience. Here we have a range of tasty morsels waiting to be served up to us. Not only do we know what we are getting but we find ourselves able to savour the pleasures of anticipation as we await the arrival of the next course.

Let's take this idea and run with it.

Turn your lesson into a menu. Present it to students at the beginning so that they know where they are going, feel special (and therefore motivated and engaged) and can enjoy the anticipation of waiting for the exciting things which are still to come.

At the start of the lesson you can either hand out lesson menus or display the delectations on the board while you talk through the various aspects of the learning which is to come.

Swap Classes

25 Find a colleague who you get on well with and arrange to swap classes with them for one lesson. It will take a bit of organising (and maybe a bit of extra planning as well) but the results are often unexpected, invigorating and fun.

Variety is the spice of life.

Nowhere is this more true than in the workplace, which can, on occasion, see the beastly figures of monotony and repetition creeping up from out of the shadows. Swapping classes is a great way to inject excitement into your familiar routine (and into students' routines).

Make a Mark

26 Just do it. Finger Lickin' Good. The Microsoft logo.

Trademarks take us to memories, connotations, images, sounds and experiences.

At lightning speed they transport us, usually conjuring up positive associations.

Create your own trademark and use it in your lessons. This doesn't have to be anything major or cheesy (though it can be if you want), just something that will instantly situate students in your lessons, making them stand out and giving them a memorable identity. Over time, this trade mark will build up a serious of positive connotations in the minds of your students.

Question Delivery

27 OK, back to questions, which are the backbone of every lesson we ever teach. In this idea we are going to use the system of postal delivery to invigorate and excite the classroom.

At the end of a lesson, hand out slips of paper to all the students in your class. Ask them to write down a question connected to the topic. Next, take a cardboard box with a hole cut in the top and ask students to post their questions through on their way out.

Next lesson, bring out the post-box and select one question at random to 'deliver' to the whole class. Read it out and ask pupils to discuss in twos or threes before sharing their ideas with the other people around them.

Say it Together

28 New words are everywhere in teaching. It's easy for us because we know them already. But those poor students of ours – so many new words to learn and remember!

Help is at hand, particularly for those trickier words we encounter.

Introduce a new word and then get your whole class to say it together. Lead them in a call and response. Try out different accents or voices, speak at different volumes and try different speeds as well. You might even like to sing the word.

All of this will help embed the term in students' memories. And if you are feeling really brave, why not throw in an action as well?

Jam and Marmalade

29 This is a great idea first passed on to me by one of the mentors I had while I was training. Jon was a brilliant teacher (and a super mentor) who was always showing me thoughtful ways to get pupils on board and to help them access the work.

One thing he did was talk about jam and marmalade. Marmalade is a big word. A bit daunting perhaps. Confusing? Maybe. Not something everyone has come across? Possibly.

Jam, on the other hand, is simple. Everyone knows jam. Jam this and jam that. Jam here and jam there.

The thing is, marmalade is just a word for orange jam.

You see how it works? It's all about using simple words pupils already know to demystify the more complex or less common ones they encounter.

Beginning. Middle. End.

30 View your lessons like stories. What's going to happen? Where's the tension? What drama is going to animate, captivate and engage your pupils?

Work out your beginning, middle and end. This will help you to ensure you have good pace. It will also make it easier to assess whether or not your pupils are making the progress you expect.

At the very end of the lesson, you might even retell what has happened in the form of a short story, helping pupils to reconceptualise their learning in narrative form – a mode of thinking long-proven to be particularly effective for storing and retaining information.

Beat the Teacher

31 Because, let's face it, who doesn't want to?

Set your students the challenge of trying to beat you. For homework they should research the topic they are currently studying before bringing two or three questions to the next lesson. They will then have a chance to ask these in an attempt to outwit you!

A couple of points to note.

Make it clear that pupils need to be able to answer their own questions.

If you have a large class you might need to collect the questions in and then choose a student to draw ones out at random before asking them to you (at which point the question-writer reveals themselves).

Secret Mission

32 Dress up any activity by writing out the instructions on a sheet of paper and placing these in a brown envelope marked: 'Top Secret,' 'Secret Mission,' or 'For Your Eyes Only.'

Pupils receive individual envelopes or work in groups and each group receives an envelope.

You can give every student the same instructions or send out a variety of different tasks.

This approach creates a sense of excitement and causes pupils to see the task differently compared to if you had introduced it as normal.

Begin with a Story

33 Stories grab our attention. They engage us in a way little else can achieve. You can use this fact by preceding activities with a story. Simply put together a short tale which leads into whatever you are asking pupils to do.

This will help enthuse and motivate your students, drawing them into the activity in question and creating a sense of purpose around what they are going to be doing.

A story could be directly connected to the learning which is to take place or it could be tangential (As I was driving into work this morning I saw a kestrel circling a field which got me thinking about...).

Choose Someone to Answer

34 Not you, the pupils.

It works like this:

When you ask a question and then ask a student for an answer, don't move straight on and pick the next person to respond. Instead, ask the pupil who has just spoken to choose the next person to answer: "Sam, can you choose the next person who is going to answer for us, please?"

This passes ownership to students, creating engagement. It also avoids bias, which may be unwittingly present, in your own selection of pupils to answer.

Bounce

35 By all means bounce around the room while you are teaching. This is bound to create an upbeat atmosphere. Although it may bring more than a few raised eyebrows if it involves a pogo stick or a space hopper.

An alternative use of bouncing sees you bouncing student answers from one pupil to the next. Here's an example:

Student 1: I think dogs are better than cats.

Teacher: Student 2, what do you think about that answer?

Student 2: Well, I'm glad you asked because I disagree actually...

The process promotes student-student discussion, minimising the role of the teacher. In addition, it trains pupils to think carefully and critically about the things their peers say.

Lego

36 Modelling things is great fun. You can build something up, creating it from scratch, and then take it apart and start all over again. Models can be of anything – the learning, concepts, events, people or ideas.

Lego is a super resource to have in your classroom for modelling. Get a boxful and then bring it out when you want students to think about what they have learnt or to reflect on the lesson as a whole.

Ask them to model something connected to what they have studied. You can walk around the room and gain a great insight into their thinking through the models they produce.

Plenary Dice

37 Plenary dice contain a series of reflective questions or tasks which can form the basis of the plenary, review activity or wrap-up you use to end your lesson.

You can buy plenary dice online (type 'plenary dice' into Google), make your own, or take two normal dice and write eleven options on the board numbered 2-12 (a student then rolls the dice to choose the plenary at random).

This is a good way to liven up the end of your lessons. You might even find students competing for the chance to roll the dice.

Make Your Own AFL Box

38 AFL means assessment for learning. Assessment for learning means giving formative feedback, eliciting information about pupils' learning and opening up success criteria. All this means raising achievement.

You can make your own AFL box containing lots of useful tools to help you embed assessment for learning in your practice. Even better, it's free! Just visit my website – www.mikegershon.com – go to the resources section and download the 'Make Your Own AFL Box' PowerPoint.

Classtools.net

39 What can I say? This is a great website. You can create all sorts of games, quizzes, activities and diagrams in a matter of seconds, ready for use in your lessons. And guess what? It's free!

Visit http://www.classtools.net/ and try it out for yourself.

Sponge Ball

40 Spongeball Squarepants? Not quite.

A sponge ball is a very handy tool to have on hand in the classroom. You can use it to choose pupils to answer questions. Students can then use it to pass the question on (by throwing the sponge ball to the next person).

You can also use it as a substitute conch in order to facilitate discussion – as in, the only person allowed to speak is the person who is holding the sponge ball.

Dingbats

41 Dingbats are images or words unusually placed or shaped which signify a particular word or phrase. You can see some at http://www.kensquiz.co.uk/table-top-quizzes/word-puzzles/dingbats.

For example, if an arrow was pointing at a space beneath the word 'hand,' you would decode this as meaning 'underhand.'

Dingbats are great for use at the beginning of a lesson. It doesn't matter if they connect to the topic or not – either way they will get pupils thinking.

Another way to use them is to have students come up with dingbats themselves and then try these out on each other. In this case it is usually most effective if pupils base their dingbats on the topic of study.

Find the Mistakes

42 Create a piece of work which relates to the learning. It should contain a number of mistakes. Divide the class into groups of three. Ask each group to stand up beside a single desk.

Walk around the room and place a copy of your piece of work face down on each desk.

When you have visited every desk return to the front of the room.

Explain that this is a race! Groups have to find a certain number of mistakes (specify the number) in the piece of work and the first group to correctly identify all the mistakes will be the winners.

Film Yourself Introducing an Activity

43 How many times do we introduce activities? Over and over again we stand at the front of the class and explain to pupils what we want them to do.

Mix things up by filming yourself introducing an activity and then playing this to students instead of standing up and telling them directly.

It should create a bit of laughter, lift the atmosphere and give a nod to the fact that you recognise things can get a bit samey at times.

Also, you might find some ways to have fun with the filming – for example by wearing a disguise or by roping in a colleague to unexpectedly introduce an activity.

Special Delivery

44 Before the lesson, find a colleague who is not teaching and give them an envelope marked 'Special Delivery.' Inside this envelope there should be a sheet of paper with instructions written on it for an activity you want your students to do.

Ask your colleague to arrive at your classroom at a specific time. They should come in dramatically and announce that an urgent letter has been sent.

You should take the letter from them and read it out to the class, who will then go ahead and do the activity contained therein.

Prezi

45 Prezi is a super alternative to PowerPoint which you can use to develop some different slides for use during your teaching. Visit the website and see how the program works - http://prezi.com/.

You might also like to introduce your students to the site and have them develop their own presentations using the resources there.

Blogs

46 The internet is awash with blogs, including many about teaching. Here are five good ones you might like to mine for great ideas:

headguruteacher.com

www.huntingenglish.com

www.coolcatteacher.com

mscassidysclass.edublogs.org

teachertoolkit.me

Noise-Makers

47 You don't always have to use your voice to get students' attention. You could use a noise-maker instead. This can be anything which makes a noise (though you might be better avoiding anything which is too loud). Here are five examples:

- A bell
- A particular sound played through the computer
- A short excerpt from a piece of music
- A triangle
- A harmonica

Teacher's Jukebox

48 I use this idea a lot with some of my older classes. It works as follows:

Set up an activity which involves students working quietly and independently, such as note-taking, question-answering or essay-writing.

Hand out a slip of paper to each pupil in the class.

Ask students to write a song choice on their slip of paper. Indicate that it must be clean and appropriate for listening to in lessons.

Collect the papers in, shuffle and then use YouTube to fire up the teacher's jukebox. This creates a nice atmosphere and is particularly good for encouraging less-focused students to remain on task (who see the whole thing as a reasonably fair trade-off).

Progress-O-Meter

49 At the start of a unit of work, draw an empty thermometer on a large piece of paper. Write the topic you are studying above this and pin it on the wall. Every lesson, invite one student to come to the front of the class and to colour in the thermometer so as to show the progress the whole class has made. By the end of the unit, the thermometer will be filled in up to the top.

You might want to mark out the different lessons you will be teaching at the start. This will then act as a guide to help students know where to colour up to. Alternatively, you can leave it blank and precede the colouring-in with a discussion during which the whole class decide together how much progress they think they have made.

Chain Reaction

50 And so we finish on a riotous activity which will get every pupil in your class up and moving, thinking, concentrating and having fun.

Students stand up and form a circle around the edges of the room.

The teacher chooses a pupil to begin. This student has to say something connected to the topic. The next student has to do the same, except they can't say what has already been said, and so forth.

Start off slowly and then encourage pupils to get faster and faster until the chain reaction is racing around the circle.

Make things even more chaotic by starting off two separate chain reactions based around two different topics.

A Brief Request

If you have found this book useful I would be delighted if you could leave a review on Amazon to let others know.

If you have any thoughts or comments, or if you have an idea for a new book in the series you would like me to write, please don't hesitate to get in touch at mike@mikegershon.com.

Finally, don't forget that you can download all my teaching and learning resources for **FREE** at www.mikegershon.com.

CPSIA information can be obtained
at www.ICGtesting.com
Printed in the USA
LVOW04s1806030216

473528LV00032B/941/P